The
1000
Questions
for Couple Book

The
1000
Questions
for Couple Book

A Time to Uncover Deeper Connections
and Improve Relationships

Be.Bull Publishing Group
Devon Abbruzzese & Mauricio Vasquez
Toronto, Canada

The 1000 Questions for Couple Book by Be.Bull Publishing Group (Aria Capri International Inc.). All Rights Reserved.

Authors:
Be.Bull Publishing Group
Devon Abbruzzese
Mauricio Vasquez
First Printing: February 2023

ISBN-978-1-990709-65-4

INTRODUCTION

We all know that a lack of open and honest communication with our partners could cause several negative repercussions.

Inadequate communication could damage trust and intimacy in a relationship. It could lead to increasing stress and anxiety, especially when dealing with serious or difficult situations. And in not-so-extreme cases, the lack of communication between partners might cause irreparable damage to their relationship and lead to a divorce.

However, before the relationships become strained, there is something that could be done. It doesn't really matter whether our relationships are in a good or bad shape, we can always try to improve it.

Better relationships can be achieved with better communication. And better communication can be achieved with better questions.

Asking questions has been, is, and always will be part of our nature. Questions allow us to gather information, learn new things, and strengthen our relationship with others.

But why is asking powerful questions important for our relationships with our partners?

Foremost, asking questions and really listening to our partners shows that we truly care. When we are at home, and we ask powerful questions to our partners, they will then know that we value them and care about their needs and opinions. Our interactions with them will always be more successful and gratifying when we are honest and intentional in acknowledging their actual needs and wants.

Asking questions helps us to align ourselves with our partner's priorities, desires, and well-being. This needs to be done with understanding and empathy towards them. We may have a general idea of what they want from us. However, it is never that easy.

What if we are making wrong assumptions and have false beliefs, and as a result, our words and actions are not really in line with what our partner is thinking and feeling? This is a recipe for a poor relationship.

Although no one can really argue the value of powerful questions, think about you and your relationship - How often do you pose meaningful questions to your partner? What questions are you asking? Are you asking too many questions that lead to arguments or fights? Are you asking judgemental questions? Are you asking too many close-ended questions that don't elicit much of a response? And finally, are you using the answers to help strengthen your communication and ultimate your relationship with your partner?

This one last question is key. If you are asking questions, and not doing anything with the responses, what is the point? It can create the opposite result you are trying to achieve. Asking questions goes far beyond exchanging information.

Here is a quote that it is relevant: "The quality of your life is determined by the quality of the questions you ask" - Tony Robbins

There is no need for you to come up with counterproductive questions or even spend minutes trying to figure out the much-needed powerful questions. The one that will transform your relationship. This book has done all the heavy lifting for you.

This book has 1000 powerful questions to reconnect with your partner and put the focus back on your relationship. This book will help you ask questions—and particularly, asking the right questions that will draw out insightful answers — answers can help you transform your relationship with your partner.

Dear valued customer,

If you would like to purchase another copy of this book for you or as a gift for a friend or family member, ***please scan this QR code.***

We thank you in advance for your purchase!

Devon & Mauricio

GUIDELINES FOR ASKING POWERFUL QUESTIONS

Read the following guidelines to learn more about asking powerful questions that unlock learning and improve relationships.

- **Effective questions are open or focused, depending on the context:** Questions that open awareness and learning are open-ended questions that cannot be answered with a yes or no. Such questions evoke deeper thinking and reflection.

- **Effective questions support learning:** You want to stimulate thinking and deepen your and your partner's understanding of what is going on. Hence, your insightful questions need to help focus your partner's attention on those aspects of the issue or situation you or your partner are dealing with that are most valuable.

- **Effective questions are asked for the benefit of your partner:** The intent is for the question to stimulate your partner's thinking and to deepen his/her understanding. It is not necessarily about you and what you want.

- **Effective questions engage a personal response:** Relationships are about an open communication, and it is the couple who create an environment for the communication to flourish. Your responsibility and privilege as part of a relationship is to engage your partner by inviting a personal response–how your partner feels, what emotions your partner is bringing to the situation. The more a question invites a personal response to a challenge or choice, the more powerful it is for facilitating learning.

- **Effective questions look beyond problems to future outcomes:** When your partner is entangled in a problem, impactful questions shift the perspective from the problem to the solution and will open new opportunities for reflection and action.

- **Effective questions facilitate openness versus defensiveness:** Impactful questions are worded and expressed with a non–judgmental tone and with open body language to prevent a defensive reaction. It is usually best to avoid questions that begin with "why" since they elicit defensive responses or explanations.

- **Effective questions co-create the best options versus manipulating outcomes:** Impactful questions are not intended to manipulate or lead your partner to the response you might think is the best response. If you want to suggest, it is best made directly as a suggestion versus a disguised directive through a question.

- **Less is more:** For powerful questions, less is usually more. Ask only one question at a time and avoid long-winded, complicated questions. A short, simple question–What is that all about? What will the consequences be? - This pulls your partner straight to the core.

TIPS FOR THE USE OF THIS BOOK

- The questions were split into 62 topics and chapters, depending on the issue or situation being discussed or faced by partners. Use this as a reference only. Many questions could fall into two or three categories.

- The best approach for any meaningful conversation is by listening. Listening to what your partner has to say with their words, emotions, physical expressions, and energy.

- For better results, tailor the questions to the specific conversation you and your partner are having.

- Combine the questions as you see fit to produce deeper insights.

- Some questions come with a couple of options to tailor them and with a blank third option to spark your creativity and come up with your own unique question.

- Asking follow-up questions is a great way to dive deeper into the conversation and uncover what really matters.

- Adapt the questions to your own vocabulary.

- Ask only one question at a time, and avoid long-winded, complicated questions.

Table of Contents

Chapter No. 1 - Questions to Ask Your Partner About Accountability

1. How do you define accountability in a (relationship/friendship/_____)?
2. How can accountability help us be better (partners/people/_____)?
3. What do you think are the most important aspects of accountability in a (relationship/family/_____)?
4. What are some practical (steps/follow-ups/_____) we can take to hold each other accountable?
5. What do you believe are the (consequences/reasons/_____) of a relationship without accountability?
6. What steps can we take together to ensure (we/you/_____) are staying accountable effectively?
7. How can we best hold each other accountable to our (goals/commitments/_____)?
8. In what ways do you (prefer/don't prefer/_____) to be held accountable?
9. What strategies come naturally to you to hold (others/myself/_____) accountable?
10. How can we support each other to be accountable in a (professional/personal/_____) setting?
11. If we hold each other accountable well, what would be the long-lasting (benefits/downside/_____) of this in our lives?

Chapter No. 2 - Questions to Ask Your Partner About Awareness

12. What do you believe is the most important aspect to be aware of throughout (life/difficult times/_____)?
13. What are the biggest obstacles that make it hard to be aware of (your surroundings/my feelings/_____)?
14. How do you stay mindful of your (thoughts/fears/_____)?
15. What are the benefits of being aware of your current (environment/reality/_____)?
16. How does awareness help us make (better decisions/new friends/_____)?
17. What are some (effects/problems/_____) you could experience if you are not aware of your thoughts and feelings?
18. How do you practice (mindfulness/gratitude/_____) in your daily life?
19. What strategies do you implement to stay (present/focused/_____)?
20. What are the warning signs you are feeling (overwhelmed/stressed/_____)?
21. What actions do you take to stay (grounded/connected/_____) to yourself?
22. What are your favorite ways to practice (self-compassion/self-care/_____)?

Chapter No. 3 - Questions to Ask Your Spouse About Being a Father

23. What is the most important thing about being a father?
24. What is the most (rewarding/inspiring/_____) part of being a father?
25. What do you believe is the most (challenging/difficult/_____) part of being a father?
26. What is the most important (lesson/skill/_____) you can teach your children?
27. How do you balance fatherhood and having a career?
28. What is the (most/least/_____) effective way to teach your children?
29. What (activities/traditions/_____) do you want to pass down to your children?
30. How do you want to be remembered as a (father/person/_____)?
31. How do you plan to involve your children in your (hobbies/interests/_____)?
32. How would you like to become involved in your children's (hobbies/homework/_____)?
33. How has becoming a father changed your perspective on (life/career/_____)?
34. What do you think is essential to remember regarding being a (good/understanding/_____) father?
35. What is the best way to show your children that you love them?
36. How do you think you can effectively support your children in their (growth/development/_____)?

37. What are the most important (life lessons/talent/_____) you will teach your children as they grow?
38. What do you believe is the (best/worst/_____) way to discipline your children?
39. What is the most (stressful/difficult/_____) part of being a father?
40. What do you think is the (least/most/_____) rewarding piece to being a father?
41. What is the worst part about being a father?
42. What is the best (way/example/_____) to show your children that you want them to succeed in school?
43. What is a good way to teach your children the important (life lessons/life skills/_____)?

Chapter No. 4 - Questions to Ask Your Spouse About Being a Mother

44. What do you find (most/least/_____) rewarding about being a mother?
45. What is the most (challenging/inspirational/_____) aspect of being a mother?
46. How has becoming a mother (changed/improved/_____) you?
47. What is one thing you wish you had known before becoming a mother?
48. What (advice/warning/_____) would you give new mothers?
49. What do you think is the most important thing to remember while raising (fearful/difficult/_____) children?

50. How do you best balance being a mother and a worker?
51. What do you believe is essential to (remember/forget/_____) when it comes to being a good mother?
52. What are the most (important/noble/_____) values to instill in your children?
53. How do you effectively balance being a mother and a wife?
54. What are the best ways to show your children (love/support/_____)?
55. What is important to remember regarding (discipline/punishment/_____)?
56. What do you (enjoy/dislike/_____) the most about being a mother?
57. How do effectively support your children's (mental/emotional well-being/_____)?
58. What do you see as the most significant (thing/sacrifice/_____) you can do as a mother?
59. How do you plan to involve your children in your (hobbies/work/_____)?
60. How do you plan to become involved in your children's (school/interests/_____)?
61. How do you handle the (expectations/pressures/_____) of motherhood?
62. How has motherhood changed your perspective on your (life/career/_____)?
63. What do you think is the best way to encourage your children to be (independent/resilient/_____)?
64. How do you plan to manage (stress/self-care/_____) as a mother?

65. How do you want to be remembered as a mother?
66. What are your (goals/dreams/_____) for your children's future?
67. How do you manage your (time/energy/_____) as a mother?
68. How can you continually improve as a mother?
69. What do you think are essential pieces of wisdom to remember when parenting?
70. What are the biggest (mistakes/wins/_____) you identify that you have made as a mother?
71. What are the most important lessons you have learned as a mother?

Chapter No. 5 - Question to Ask Your Partner About Belief

72. What is your core belief system?
73. What (values/principles/_____) do you live out every day?
74. How would you define the purpose of life?
75. What do you think is the most important (aspect/thing/_____) in life?
76. What is the key to (happiness/fulfillment/_____)?
77. What is the most essential thing to remember about (life/death/_____)?
78. What do you consider being the ultimate (goal/aim/_____) in life?
79. What is the most fundamental thing to (believe/remember/_____) about being human?

80. How do you determine the (difference/similarities/_____) between right and wrong?
81. What do you always keep in mind for believing in something?
82. How do you explain the difference between faith and belief?
83. How do (beliefs/attitudes/_____) shape our lives?
84. How do your beliefs shape your (decision making/habits/_____)?
85. What beliefs have you held in the past that you have since changed your mind about?
86. What beliefs do you think are still widely (accepted/embraced/_____) in society today that are wrong?
87. What (incorrect/unfunded/_____) beliefs do people hold that you think are particularly damaging?
88. How do you handle circumstances when your beliefs are (challenged/inconsistent/_____)?
89. How do your beliefs influence your relationship with (me/others/_____)?

Chapter No. 6 - Questions to Ask Your Partner About Blind Spots

90. What could be your (biggest/detrimental/_____) blind spots?
91. How do you think your blind spots have impacted (your/my life/_____)?
92. How do you effectively (identify/address/_____) your blind spots?

93. Have your blind spots ever affected your relationship with (family members/me/_____)?
94. What have you learned is essential to (remember/keep in mind/_____) when facing your blind spots?
95. How do you believe your blind spots have impacted your (career/personal life/_____)?
96. How can I support you when you are impacted by your blind spots?

Chapter No. 7 - Questions to Ask Your Partner About Brothers or Sisters

97. How many siblings do you have?
98. How would you describe your relationship with your (siblings/parents/_____)?
99. What is the most (memorable/fun/_____) moment you have shared with your siblings?
100. What do you think is the (best/worst/_____) part of having a brother or sister?
101. Do you have any (funny/horrible/_____) stories about you and your siblings?
102. What do you believe is the biggest (challenge/problem/_____) of having siblings?
103. How have your siblings had a (good/bad/_____) influence on who you are today?
104. What qualities do you (admire/like/_____) most in a brilliant brother or sister?
105. What do you think makes a (respectful/disrespectful/_____) brother or sister?
106. How should a good brother or sister treat their (siblings/parents/_____)?

107. How close are you to your siblings?
108. What are the benefits of having an awesome brother or sister?
109. What is the ideal way to handle (disagreements/fights/_____) with your siblings?
110. Have your siblings ever behaved so poorly that it affected your relationship with them?
111. What do you think caused your brother or sister to behave that way?
112. How did you react to your brother's or sister's (bad/disrespectful/_____) behavior?
113. What was your parents' response to your brother's or sister's bad behavior?
114. Do you believe your brother or sister's poor behavior had any lasting effects on (you/your family/_____)?

Chapter No. 8 - Questions to Ask Your Partner About Change

115. What (big/small/_____) changes have you recently experienced in your life?
116. How do you feel about change?
117. What is the most (important/inspiring/_____) thing to keep in mind regarding change?
118. What are your (strengths/weaknesses/_____) when adapting to changes?
119. In what ways is change (beneficial/detrimental/_____)?
120. What do you think most people struggle with the most when faced with changes?
121. How do you believe people can ideally prepare for change?

122. What changes do you want to see happen in (your own life/my life/_____)?
123. What (steps/drastic measures/_____) do you plan to take to make those changes happen?
124. What are the biggest (obstacles/opportunities/_____) to achieving these changes?
125. How can (your family/I/_____) support you as you work on making these changes?
126. What are you looking forward to the most (after/while/_____) these changes are implemented?
127. Do you see any change coming (this year/next year/_____) that will be particularly difficult?

Chapter No. 9 - Questions to Ask Your Partner About Children

128. What activities do you (enjoy/not enjoy/_____) doing with children?
129. How do you handle children's (discipline/ unreasonable demands/_____)?
130. What is the best way to help children (learn to read/deal with everyday anger/_____)?
131. What do you do if a child is being (disruptive/challenging/_____)?
132. What is the most important (life lesson/subject/_____) to teach children?
133. How do you approach a (disagreement/fight/_____) between yourself and children?
134. How can we best foster (creativity/growth mindset/_____) in children?

135. What are the essential (values/habits/_____) we need to teach our children?
136. How do we show our children we are a unified team?
137. What can we (do/say/_____) to show respect for each other daily?
138. How can we (share/exemplify/_____) our commitment to our relationship with our children?
139. In what ways can we show our children that we are (responsible/reliable/_____)?
140. How will our children see we are open to (learning/growing/_____) together?
141. What can our children do to improve their (grades/attitude towards us/_____)?
142. How can we support our children to reach their (goals/potential/_____)?
143. What type of impact do our children have in (the local community/our family/_____)?
144. What do you think is important to teach our children, so they have a positive influence (in the world/at the school/_____)?
145. How do we encourage our children to make (positive changes/more of an effort/_____)?

Chapter No. 10 - Questions to Ask Your Partner About Codependency

146. How would you (define/not define/_____) codependency?
147. What are some signs of codependency in a (healthy/unhealthy/_____) relationship?
148. How can codependency affect a relationship?

149. What do you believe are the primary (causes/consequences/_____) of codependency?
150. What can (I/we/_____) do now to prevent codependency in our relationship?
151. What is important to (remember/do/_____) when facing codependency?
152. What do you think are the (benefits/drawbacks/_____) of a codependent relationship?
153. How can we create a healthier balance between our individual needs and our relationship's needs?
154. What can we focus on more to (improve/avoid/_____) codependency in our relationship?
155. How can we more effectively communicate our (needs/feelings/_____) to each other?
156. What (boundaries/habits/_____) are necessary for us to set in our relationship?
157. How do you feel about our relationship as it (is now/was before/_____)?
158. How can I support you through the (changes/improvements/_____) we make to our relationship?
159. What do you believe are (important/required/_____) aspects of a healthy relationship?
160. How can I help you become (more/less/_____) independent in our relationship?
161. What are the benefits of having a healthy relationship?
162. How can I help you feel more secure in our relationship apart from codependency?

Chapter No. 11 - Questions to Ask Your Partner About Commitment

163. How would you (define/don't define/_____) commitment in your own words?
164. How do you show your commitment to a (relationship/friendship/_____)?
165. What are your expectations for commitment within our (relationship/family/_____)?
166. How do you approach disagreements regarding commitments to come to an understanding?
167. What do you think is the most (important/underrated/_____) aspect of a committed relationship?
168. What actions would you take if there are (concerns/arguments/_____) about commitment in a relationship?
169. What is the key to a (successful/committed/_____) relationship?
170. How is loyalty different from commitment?
171. How do you show loyalty to your (partner/coworkers/_____)?
172. How do you (maintain/improve/_____) commitment in a relationship over time?
173. What (qualities/traits/_____) does a loyal partner possess?
174. What would you do if you found your (partner/employee/_____) was not loyal to you?
175. What do you do to show loyalty publicly in a relationship?

176. Have you ever made a (fake/unrealistic/_____) commitment, and why?
177. How did you think it would benefit you?
178. How did it would affect the other person?
179. What did you believe would happen if your (friend/parent/_____) found out about the false commitment?
180. How did you feel after the other person discovered it was false?
181. What did you learn from the overall experience, and would you do it again?
182. What advice would you give to someone who is contemplating entering a fake commitment?

Chapter No. 12 - Questions to Ask Your Partner About Communication

183. How can we effectively communicate our (needs/feelings/_____) to each other?
184. What expectations do (we/you/_____) have for how often we should communicate?
185. How can we ensure both of us are (heard/understood/_____)?
186. Do we have any topics that are (off-limits/required/_____) for discussion?
187. How can (your family/I/_____) make sure you feel heard and understood?
188. What can I do to better (communicate with/support/_____) you while you are feeling overwhelmed or stressed?

189. What is the most important thing for us to prioritize right now?
190. What steps can we take to create a safe space to talk openly and honestly about our feelings?
191. How do you (prefer/not prefer/_____) to receive constructive feedback?
192. What is the (most/least/_____) effective way for me to communicate my expectations to you?

Chapter No. 13 - Questions to Ask Your Partner About Conflict

193. What is the best way we can (resolve/avoid/_____) a conflict?
194. How can we both achieve our desired outcome in a (situation/fight/_____)?
195. What do you believe is the (root cause/consequence/_____) of the conflict?
196. How can we most effectively communicate our (needs/wants/_____)?
197. How do you suggest we move forward?
198. What compromises can (we/you/_____) make to reach a resolution?
199. How do you feel when a conflict arises (in our relationship/at work/_____)?
200. What are some common causes of conflict in our (relationship/family/_____)?
201. What are some ways we can prevent (conflicts/fights/_____) from escalating?
202. How do you feel about seeking outside (help/support/_____) for conflicts in our relationship?

203. How can I show I hear you and understand you?
204. How do you feel about taking a break during a heated conflict to cool down and come back to it later?
205. Can you share an example of a conflict we've had in the past and how we resolved it?
206. What is the best way to resolve conflicts with (you/others/_____)?
207. How can we work together to create a positive environment for (you/both of us/_____) following a disagreement?
208. Do you require space during a conflict, or do you prefer to address it head-on?
209. What are some ground rules we can put in place to respect each other's (opinions/feelings/_____) during a conflict?
210. What do you think is the ideal way to approach difficult conversations?

Chapter No. 14 - Questions to Ask Your Partner About Creativity

211. What is the most important (element/criteria/_____) of creativity?
212. What are the biggest (challenges/opportunities/_____) you face while being creative?
213. What is (rewarding/challenging/_____) about engaging in creativity?
214. What skills are required to be creative?
215. What are the specific (tools/moments/_____) needed to enjoy creativity fully?

216. What kinds of (habits/talents/_____) encourage creativity?
217. What specific creative (activities/games/_____) bring you the most joy?
218. What is the key to being (joyful/excited/_____) during creativity?
219. What do you think are the benefits of engaging in creative activities?
220. What is your favorite way to (display/develop/_____) your creativity?
221. How can you stay (motivated/inspired/_____) to be creative?

Chapter No. 15 - Questions to Ask Your Partner About Date Nights

222. What type of date nights do you (enjoy/dislike/_____) the most?
223. What makes a date night (successful/unsuccessful/_____)?
224. What are some of your favorite date night activities?
225. What is most important to remember for (success/enjoyment/_____) when planning a date night?
226. What do you think is the best way to make a date night (special/more meaningful/_____)?
227. What is the best manner to make a date night (memorable/forgettable/_____)?
228. How often do you think a couple should have date nights?

229. What is your favorite type of (restaurant/bar/_____) to go to on a date night?
230. What is the most (memorable/fun/_____) date night you have ever had?
231. How important is it to mix things up and try new things on date night?
232. What are some of your favorite date night (ideas/games/_____) we should try?
233. How do you handle any (budget/time/_____) constraints when it comes to planning date nights?
234. What would make a date night boring?
235. What would you like to do differently to make our next date night more (exciting/romantic/_____)?
236. How do you think date nights can contribute to a healthy relationship?
237. What do you think would be a great way to turn a boring date night into an (exciting/adventurous/_____) one?
238. How do you think date nights can help us overcome any (issues/ challenges/_____) in our relationship?

Chapter No. 16 - Questions to Ask Your Partner About Death

239. How did (they/your parents/_____) die?
240. What were their last (words/actions/_____)?
241. Did they have any final wishes?
242. What are your favorite (memories/experiences/_____) with them?
243. What (hobbies/interest/_____) did they share with you?
244. What (beliefs/values/_____) did they hold dear?

245. What hopes and dreams did they (fulfill/not fulfill/_____) in life?
246. What were their proudest accomplishments?
247. What were their favorite places to visit, and why?
248. What experiences did they enjoy most?
249. How can we prepare for the death of a loved one?
250. What are (legal/financial/_____) considerations when someone dies?
251. How can we (support/comfort/_____) each other during the grieving process?
252. What are some loving ways to (honor/remember/_____) a deceased loved one?
253. What types of funeral services are available?
254. What type of support can I offer that will help (you/our family/_____) the most?
255. Do you want to talk about your loved one?
256. What are some ways we can honor the memory of our loved one?
257. What steps should we take to cope with (their/our/_____) grief and sadness?
258. Is there something special we can do to share our favorite memories of our loved one?
259. In what ways should we grieve healthily (together/separately/_____)?
260. What are some manners we can help (each other/others/_____) heal?

Chapter No. 17 - Questions to Ask Your Partner About Decisions

261. What major factors do you consider when making (decisions/a new decision/_____)?
262. When it comes to making (a decision/a change in your life/_____), how do you weigh the pros and cons?
263. What do you do when you face a difficult (personal/business/_____) decision?
264. If you disagree with someone, how do you handle making (decisions together/mistakes/_____)?
265. How do you decide when you are (confused/uncertain of the choice/_____)?
266. How do you approach decision-making when you are feeling (overwhelmed/unsure/_____)?
267. How do you involve your (partner/colleagues/_____) in the decision-making process?
268. How do you weigh the risk of a decision before you make it?
269. How do you make decisions that affect the future of (your life/our relationship/_____)?
270. What are the most important things to consider when making a decision that affects (both partners/your partner only/_____)?
271. What do you do when you think you've made a (poor/regrettable/_____) choice?
272. What is the (best/worst/_____) decision you have ever made?
273. What lessons did you learn from it?
274. How did it impact (your/my/_____) life?

275. If you could go back and make the decision again, what would you do differently?
276. What advice would you give to (your children/me/_____) who is considering making a similar decision?
277. How have you (taken steps/made decisions/_____) to ensure you don't make the same mistake again?

Chapter No. 18 - Questions to Ask Your Partner About Divorce

278. What are the (legal/emotional/_____) grounds for a divorce?
279. What is the process for filing for divorce?
280. What would the financial implications be of divorce?
281. What are the potential tax implications of divorce?
282. How would our shared assets and debts be divided?
283. How would we determine child custody and visitation?
284. How would child support be determined?
285. Have you ever considered divorce?
286. What would be the main reasons that would lead (you/us/_____) to consider divorce?
287. What are the potential (good/bad/_____) outcomes of a divorce?
288. How do you think our (family/friends/_____) would react to a divorce?
289. What are your thoughts on the concept of "irreconcilable differences" in a marriage?
290. What are your options for spousal support during a divorce?
291. What are your thoughts on couples (therapy/counseling/_____)?

292. How do you think we can work on resolving conflicts in our relationship?

Chapter No. 19 - Questions to Ask Your Partner About Education

293. What was your favorite (subject/class/_____) in school?
294. What was the (easiest/most challenging/_____) class you ever took?
295. What important (lesson/competence/_____) did you learn from your educational experiences?
296. What is the most important subject to learn in (school/university/_____)?
297. What is the (most/least/_____) effective way to motivate students to learn?
298. What do you think are the biggest (challenges/opportunities/_____) facing education today?
299. What do you believe are the most important (skills/habits/_____) to learn during the educational years?
300. What are three essential elements for a high-quality (education/learning experience/_____)?
301. What are the largest (challenges/opportunities/_____) for providing a high-quality education to people?
302. What strategies could our (society/government/_____) employ to improve the quality of education?
303. How can technology be used to improve the quality of education?
304. What are your educational (goals/aspirations/_____)?

305. How do you plan to prioritize (education/learning/_____) in our relationship?
306. How do you plan to (support/encourage/_____) each other's educational goals?
307. How will education impact our future together?
308. What do you see as the biggest (challenges/opportunities/_____) that educators face in providing the best quality education to students?
309. How can we support educators?

Chapter No. 20 - Questions to Ask Your Partner About Emotional Intimacy

310. What can I offer so that (we/you/_____) both feel emotionally connected?
311. How can I best support you when you are feeling (down/overwhelmed/_____)?
312. What are the ways you express your (love/appreciation/_____) for me?
313. What is essential to creating a strong emotional connection in our relationship?
314. How do you regularly express your (emotions/frustrations/_____)?
315. How do you feel when we (share/don't share/_____) emotional intimacy?
316. How do you feel when we (lack/enjoy/_____) emotional intimacy?
317. What are some things that make it easier for (us/you/_____) to achieve emotional intimacy?

Chapter No. 21 - Questions family Your Partner About Emotions

318. What emotions do you primarily (experience/suffer/_____) most days?
319. How do you typically (express/hide/_____) your emotions?
320. What do you do when you feel (overwhelmed/sad/_____)?
321. What does it look like when you feel you can't control your emotions?
322. How do you handle difficult emotions, such as anger or sadness?
323. Is there someone you go to when you need to talk about your emotions?
324. What do you think are the most important emotions to express in a healthy relationship?
325. How do you express your emotions in (healthy/unhealthy/_____) ways?
326. How do you like to receive emotional support from your partner?
327. What actions (do/could/_____) you take to care of your own emotional well-being?
328. What causes you to recognize when you are experiencing (overwhelm/ stress/_____)?
329. What strategies do you (use/don't use/_____) to manage your emotions healthily?
330. What are some (unhealthy/negative/_____) emotions you experienced in the past?
331. How do you usually handle feeling (negative/positive/_____) emotions?

332. How should we handle feelings of vulnerability in a relationship?
333. How do you feel about expressing emotions in (public/private/_____)?
334. How do you feel about (crying/showing vulnerability/_____) in front of your partner?
335. What steps do you take to help yourself feel (better/happier/_____) when you are feeling unhealthy emotions?

Chapter No. 22 - Questions to Ask Your Partner About Excitement

336. What things (excite/stimulate/_____) you the most?
337. When you are feeling (excited/happy/_____), what do you always do?
338. What is the most (exciting/memorable/_____) thing you've ever done?
339. What is the most exciting thing (you have/you haven't/_____) experienced?
340. What is the key to maintaining excitement about (life/sex/life)?
341. How can someone create excitement in (their/my/_____) life?
342. What activities give you the most excitement?
343. What steps do you take to stay (motivated/excited/_____) about life?
344. What is the most (exciting/boring/_____) thing about life that everyone experiences?
345. What are the (best/worst/_____) ways to create excitement in your life?

346. What excites you the (most/least/_____) in a relationship?

347. Are there activities that we can do (together/separately/_____) to bring our relationship more excitement?

Chapter No. 23 - Questions to Ask Your Partner About Family

348. What is your earliest memory of your family?

349. What (values/fears/_____) were instilled in you during your childhood from your family?

350. What is your favorite family (tradition/memory/_____)?

351. What do you believe is an important lesson you learned from your family?

352. What is the most meaningful thing your family has done for you?

353. What do you appreciate the (most/least/_____) about your family?

354. What makes your family (unique/strong/_____)?

355. How would you define a (happy/sad/_____) family?

356. What are three of your favorite (family/childhood/_____) memories?

357. What do you believe are essential (values/experiences/_____) for a family to have?

358. What are the most important things for a family to (do/achieve/_____) together?

359. What are the topics for a family to (talk/forget/_____) about?

360. Are there specific things any family should share with one another?

361. What do you see as the principal causes for (happiness/unhappiness/_____) in our family?
362. How could our family (work/behave/_____) together to create a more positive environment?
363. What are our family's biggest (challenges/opportunities/_____) for resolving conflicts?
364. How could our family communicate more effectively to express our (feelings/concerns/_____) with each other?
365. How can your family appreciate me more?

Chapter No. 24 - Questions to Ask Your Partner About Fear

366. What is the (scariest/worst/_____) thing you have experienced?
367. What is your (greatest/silliest/_____) fear?
368. How can I help when you are feeling (afraid/anxious/_____)?
369. How do you best cope with (fear/anxiety/_____)?
370. What would you say to encourage (someone/your children/_____) who is facing her/his fears?
371. What do you (do/overcome/_____) to conquer your fears?
372. What is your most (irrational/scariest/_____) fear?
373. When did this fear first become apparent?
374. Does this fear affect your (life/profession/_____) regularly?
375. How do you (cope with/conquer/_____) this fear?
376. Do you feel (justified/unjustified/_____) in having this fear?
377. Have you ever sought professional help to conquer it?

378. Is there (someone/something/_____) that causes the fear to appear?
379. Do you think this fear will ever go away?
380. What are some rational fears (you/I/_____) have?
381. How do you cope with these rational fears?
382. Do you have any steps you take to (manage/avoid/_____) your rational fears?
383. What are some (similarities/differentiating factors/_____) between rational and irrational fears?
384. What are the (benefits/limitations/_____) of having rational fears?
385. Do you believe rational fears can influence you to make (better/worst/_____) decisions?
386. Are rational fears (appropriate/inappropriate/_____) in certain situations?

Chapter No. 25 - Questions to Ask Your Partner About Feelings

387. What emotions do you experience (frequently/the least/_____)?
388. What do you do when you are feeling (overwhelmed/burdened/_____)?
389. Do you feel (free/shy/_____) to express your feelings to others?
390. Do you do anything specific when you are feeling down/stressed out/_____)?
391. How do you handle feeling (difficult/irrational/_____) emotions?
392. If you feel angry, what do you (do/don't do/_____) to calm down?

393. How do you best show (love/affection/_____)?
394. How do you handle feelings of (anxiety/loneliness/_____)?
395. What are the most important components to a relationship with (healthy/joyful/_____) emotions?
396. How do you think we can best communicate what we are feeling to (each other/others/_____)?
397. What are the (benefits/opportunities/_____) of expressing our feelings openly and honestly?
398. How can we support (each other/others/_____) when we are feeling down or overwhelmed?
399. What should we remember when it comes to (managing/expressing/_____) our emotions?
400. What are some (unhealthy/healthy/_____) feelings you have experienced recently?
401. How do you usually cope with (unhealthy/morbid/_____) feelings in a healthy manner?
402. Can you identify the (root causes/consequences/_____) of your unhealthy feelings?
403. What are the most (effective/difficult/_____) ways to manage unhealthy feelings?
404. What is essential to keep in mind when experiencing (unhealthy/sad/_____) feelings?
405. What impact do your unhealthy feelings have on (others/me/_____)?

Chapter No. 26 - Questions to Ask Your Partner About Fighting

406. What are some (strategies/resources/_____) to resolve conflicts without resorting to fighting?
407. How can we communicate more effectively when we (disagree/fight/_____)?
408. What are some (healthy/unhealthy/_____) ways to express anger and frustrations?
409. What strategies can we implement to prevent future arguments from (escalating/happening/_____)?
410. What are signs that a disagreement is becoming (unhealthy/absurd/_____)?
411. How can we create a safe space to talk about our differing opinions?
412. What do you need during a (fight/argument/_____)?
413. How can (I/your family/_____) help you feel better during a fight?
414. What is the best way to come to a resolution after fighting?
415. What do you believe is the root cause of the (issue/fight/_____)?
416. How can we effectively prevent an argument from happening again?
417. What is a suitable compromise we can both agree to?
418. What should we put all our focus on right now?
419. What are some (rules/belief/_____) we should consider for a fair fight?
420. How do you communicate when you are (upset/frustrated/_____)?

421. How do you repair the relationship after a fight?
422. What can we do to maintain a healthy level of (honesty/respect/_____) during a fight?
423. What are some things that you don't feel comfortable (discussing/sharing/_____) during a fight?
424. How do you determine when it's time to move on from a fight?
425. How can I best show you I'm sorry and ask for forgiveness?

Chapter No. 27 - Questions to Ask Your Partner About Fitness

426. What are your (fitness/health/_____) goals for this year?
427. How can (I/your family/_____) support you in achieving your fitness goals?
428. What types of (physical activities/exercises/_____) do you enjoy doing?
429. Would you like to try a new (workout class/gym/_____) together?
430. What are some healthy (meals/snacks/_____) you would like to incorporate into the diet for our family?
431. Can we set achievable and realistic (fitness/nutrition/_____) goals together?
432. Are there any specific (habits/routines/_____) that you would like to change to improve your health?
433. How can (I/your family/_____) encourage and motivate you to stick to your fitness plan?
434. Are there any (barriers/challenges/_____) that you foresee in reaching your fitness?

435. How can we overcome any barrier or challenge that (you/we/_____) might face?
436. What is at stake if you don't improve your fitness?

Chapter No. 28 - Questions to Ask Your Partner About Flow

437. What does the term flow mean to (you/I/_____)?
438. How can (you/I/_____) identify when you are in a state of flow?
439. What activities help you easily (enter/lose/_____) a flow state?
440. How do you best stay focused and in the flow?
441. If you feel (stuck/excited/_____), what strategies do you implement to return to the flow?
442. Can (you/I/_____) use flow to help you achieve your goals?

Chapter No. 29 - Questions to Ask Your Partner About Friendships

443. What important (qualities/attributes/_____) do you look for in a friend?
444. What is the (ideal/worst/_____) way to handle a disagreement with friends?
445. What do you think creates a (strong/weak/_____) friendship?
446. How do you show your friends that you care about them and their well-being?
447. What actions do you take when a friend is going through a difficult time?

448. What is your (response/behavior/_____) when a friend is not being supportive of you?

449. How do you (maintain/improve/_____) your friendships while in a relationship?

450. How do you feel about me having friends of the opposite sex?

451. How should a good friend treat (you/me/_____)?

452. What are the (benefits/privileges/_____) of having good friends?

453. How do you handle any (jealousy/insecurity/_____) related to your friends?

454. What do you think are the signs of a (bad/unhealthy/_____) friendship?

455. How do you handle (boundaries/privacy/_____) for friendships?

456. What behaviors are unacceptable in a friendship?

457. How do you feel about (meeting/getting to know/_____) my friends?

458. What do you think is an (appropriate/inappropriate/_____) boundary with group activities or outings with friends?

459. How do you feel about (maintaining/discarding/_____) friendships from previous relationships?

460. In what way should (you/me/_____) prioritize your friends and their needs in relation to our relationship?

Chapter No. 30 - Questions to Ask Your Partner About Fulfillment

461. What is the most important (factor/consideration/_____) in achieving fulfillment?

462. What do you think is the biggest (opportunity/obstacle/_____) in the way of true fulfillment?
463. What is the (best/worst/_____) way to measure fulfillment?
464. What do you see as the (most/least/_____) rewarding part of achieving fulfillment?
465. What is necessary to remember while striving for fulfillment?
466. What (does/doesn't/_____) ultimate fulfillment look like to you?

Chapter No. 31 - Questions to Ask Your Partner About Goals

467. What are some of your short-term goals?
468. What are your long-term goals?
469. What steps do you take to achieve your goals?
470. What (obstacles/difficult people/_____) have you encountered along the way to your goals?
471. How do you stay motivated to reach your (short/long-term/_____) goals)?
472. What is the best (attitude/mindset/_____) to adopt in order to achieve your goals?
473. What is our (primary/secondary/_____) goal that we are achieving together?
474. What steps do you believe are (necessary/unnecessary/_____) to reach our goal?
475. To achieve our goal, what (resources/tools/_____) are needed?

476. What do you think are the biggest (opportunities/challenges/_____) facing us as we work toward our goals?
477. Do you have suggestions for how we can stay (motivated/accountable/_____)?
478. How should we measure our (progress/results/_____)?
479. What are some ideas of (rewards/fun times/_____) that we could enjoy once we achieve our goal?

Chapter No. 32 - Questions to Ask Your Partner About Gratitude

480. What are some ways we can show gratitude to (each other/our family/_____)?
481. How can we express our sincere (appreciation/love/_____) for each other?
482. What can I do to make you feel valued?
483. How can we ensure we both feel gratitude in our (relationship/family/_____)?
484. What creative ways come to mind where we can show our gratitude for (each other/other/_____)?
485. How can we maintain a feeling of thankfulness for each other?
486. What do you appreciate the most about (me/us/_____)?
487. How do (I/we/_____) regularly strengthen our relationship?
488. What do you think (I/we/_____) can do to better our relationship?
489. What do I do that makes you feel incredibly (loved/unloved/_____)?

490. How do I make you feel the (most/least/_____) respected?

491. In what way do I support you the best?

Chapter No. 33 - Questions to Ask Your Partner About Habits

492. What do your daily habits (look/don't look/_____) like?

493. Do you have any (bad/unhealthy/_____) habits that you would like to break?

494. What are some (good/new/_____) habits that you are proud of?

495. How have your habits (changed/deteriorated/_____) over the years for good or bad?

496. What are the benefits of having (good/positive/_____) habits?

497. What do you think are some (reasons/consequences/_____) for continuing bad habits?

498. How do your habits affect (your family, your life/_____)?

499. What good habits took a long period of time to (develop/start with/_____)?

500. How do you stay motivated to maintain your (new/good/_____) habits?

501. What habits are the most important for (you/me/_____) to have?

502. How essential to your day are your habits?

503. What advice would you offer (someone/your children/_____) who is developing good habits?

504. How do your habits affect our relationship?

505. How do you handle it when (your family/I/_____) bring up concerns about your habits?
506. What do you think is the most (challenging/beneficial/_____) part to breaking a bad habit?
507. What strategies have been (successful/unsuccessful/_____) in the past when you broke a bad habit?
508. What do you think is (essential/important/_____) successful to effectively break a bad habit?
509. What are some habits that you have that (positively/negatively/_____) contribute to our relationship?

Chapter No. 34 - Questions to Ask Your Spouse About His/Her Day

510. What was the (highlight/best/_____) of your day?
511. What was the most (challenging/boring/_____) part of your day, and why?
512. What did you learn today?
513. What made you (laugh/cry/_____)?
514. What was the (most/least/_____) rewarding part of your day?
515. How did you make your most difficult decision today?
516. What was the most (interesting/superficial/_____) conversation you had?
517. Did anything unexpected happen today?
518. What do (other/I/_____) might think it was a taught part of your day?
519. What was the most rewarding part of your day?

520. What is a (challenge/risk/_____) you normally face every day?
521. How did you handle a challenge you encounter?
522. What did you learn from a challenging (experience/person/_____)?
523. Do you wish you would have addressed an (issue/conversation/_____) differently today?
524. What did you do to take care of (yourself/myself/_____) today?
525. How can I (support/help/_____) you through this challenging day?
526. What was the best part of your day?
527. What made you (smile/think/_____)?
528. What is one good thing you (did/didn't do/_____) today?
529. What was an exciting thing you (experienced/didn't experience/_____) today?
530. How can I make your days better?
531. What is one thing you wish you could (forget/remember/_____) about today?
532. What do you think was the most enjoyable part of your day?
533. How can you make your own day more (fulfilling/interesting/_____)?
534. What was the most (meaningful/lively/_____) moment of the day?
535. What was the most (fascinating/creepy/_____) thing that happened today?

Chapter No. 35 - Questions to Ask Your Partner About His/Her Father/Mother

536. What is your (favorite/least-liked/_____) memory of your father/mother?
537. What have you learned from your father/mother?
538. What do you wish you could have learned from your father/mother?
539. What was your father/mother like when you were (growing up/misbehaving/_____)?
540. What is the most important (lesson/mindset/_____) your father/mother taught you?
541. What do you (admire/don't admire/_____) about your father/mother?
542. What (memories/activities/_____) do you have of you and your father/mother doing things together?
543. What is an example of a (time/topic/_____) you and your father/mother disagreed?
544. How would you describe your (relationship/arguments/_____) with your father/mother?
545. How has your relationship with your father/mother evolved over time?
546. What was the (best/worst/_____) advice your father/mother ever gave you?
547. What normal activity was the most (fun/boring/_____) that you did with your father/mother?
548. How does your father/mother handle (conflicts/disagreements/_____)?
549. How does your father/mother express (love/respect/_____)?

550. How does your father/mother make financial decisions?
551. What is the best advice your father/mother has ever given you when you were a child?
552. What is the most meaningful thing your father/mother has ever (said/done/_____) for you?
553. What is the (funniest/happiest/_____) memory you have of your father/mother?
554. In what ways do your father/mother handle (communication/expressions of emotions/_____)?
555. What is the (best/worst/_____) thing about your relationship with your father/mother?

Chapter No. 36 - Questions to Ask Your Partner About Infidelity

556. (What/who/_____) led to the infidelity?
557. How can we rebuild trust between us?
558. What do we need to do to prevent this from happening again?
559. Are there any ways I can help you heal?
560. Have you ever been unfaithful in a relationship before?
561. What can we do to strengthen our relationship?
562. Have you ever been tempted to cheat on me?
563. What are your (thoughts/perceptions/_____) on open relationships?
564. How would (you/we/_____) handle it if one of us had a one-night stand?
565. What are your (boundaries/thoughts/_____) when it comes to interacting with people of the opposite sex?
566. Have you ever had (feelings/desires/_____) for someone else while in a relationship with me?

567. What (steps/commitments/_____) should be taken to regain trust and show faithfulness again?
568. How can we move forward after this?

Chapter No. 37 - Questions to Ask Your Partner About Insecurity

569. What are the (warning signs/reasons/_____) of insecurity in a relationship?
570. How can I help (you/myself/_____) feel more secure in our relationship?
571. What can I do to build (trust/loyalty/_____) between us in our relationship?
572. How can you understand your feelings about insecurity better?
573. What are the (root causes/consequences/_____) of your insecurities?
574. How do (you/I/_____) manage your insecurities?
575. What strategies do you implement to build self-confidence?
576. How do you (prefer/not prefer/_____) to communicate your feelings of insecurity in a constructive way?
577. What can we do together to create a safe and supportive environment for (each other/you/_____)?
578. How do you feel when I express my own insecurities?
579. How can we grow (understanding/compassion/_____) with each other?
580. What are some common triggers that bring up feelings of insecurity for (you/me/_____)?
581. How can we create a plan to address (our/your/_____) insecurities together?

582. What resources are available to us that we can use to work through our insecurities?

Chapter No. 38 - Questions to Ask Your Partner About Intimacy

583. What do you find most (fulfilling/sexy/_____) about being intimate with me?
584. What is a (vital/underrated/_____) element of a healthy, intimate relationship?
585. What are the most important (things/toys/_____) to enjoy when you are intimate with me?
586. How do you think a couple can handle (differences/changes/_____) in their intimate desires or needs?
587. What is imperative to keep in mind (during/before/_____) intimate times together?
588. What makes us (special/adorable/_____) as a couple?
589. What do you appreciate the most about (me/us/_____)?
590. What do you define as the most important (thing/attribute/_____) in a close relationship?
591. What are the best ways to show each other (love/passion/_____)?
592. What are the most effective ways to communicate with each other?
593. When we face intimate (challenges/disappointments/_____), what do we both need to remember?
594. What is the (most/least/_____) attractive aspect of me?
595. What is the most important part of a relationship?

596. How could (we/you/_____) avoid escalating our fights?
597. What do you feel is a meaningful thing I do for you?
598. What would you want me to do for you as a (romantic/generous/_____) gesture?
599. What can I focus on to make you feel (loved/appreciated/_____)?

Chapter No. 39 - Questions to Ask Your Partner About Jealousy

600. What are some things that trigger (my/your/_____) jealousy?
601. How do (I/you/_____) react when you feel jealous?
602. How can I help you feel more (secure/faithful/_____) in our relationship?
603. What steps can (we/you/_____) take together to address any conflict that arises from jealousy?
604. How do you differentiate between healthy and unhealthy jealousy in a relationship?
605. How can we communicate effectively when (you/me/_____) is feeling jealous?
606. What do you think are some (root causes/outcomes/_____) of your feelings of jealousy?
607. What is the (most/least/_____) supportive response I can give if you express you are feeling jealous?
608. What (actions/strategies/_____) would help us better manage our jealousy in our relationship?
609. How can we work to (prevent/resolve/_____) jealousy from affecting our relationship?

Chapter No. 40 - Questions to Ask Your Partner About Keeping Things Exciting

610. What is something you would like to try that we haven't done before?
611. What activity would like to do (together/separately/_____) that we haven't done in a while?
612. How can we keep the spark alive in our relationship?
613. What are some ways we can (surprise each other/keep things fresh/_____)?
614. What do you think is important to maintain (excitement/love/_____) in a relationship?
615. What would make our relationship more exciting?
616. How can we strengthen our (relationship/family/_____)?
617. How can we keep our (communication/loyalty/_____) strong and exciting?
618. How can we make sure we take time for ourselves and each other to keep things exciting?
619. In what ways can we make our relationship (more exciting/better/_____)?
620. How can (I/you/_____) be more romantic in our relationship?
621. What (adventures/learning experiences/_____) do you want to go on together?

Chapter No. 41 - Questions to Ask Your Partner About Leadership Style

622. What do you believe are the most important (qualities/aptitudes/_____) of a good leader?
623. How do you (motivate/inspire/_____) our family?
624. What strategies have you implemented to ensure that everyone is working together effectively?
625. How do you approach difficult (conversations/fights/_____) with each family member?
626. What is one leadership quality you are working toward?
627. How do you handle (disagreements/jealously/_____) between family members?
628. What do you identify on you that sets you apart as a leader?

Chapter No. 42 - Questions to Ask your Partner About Life

629. What do you think are the most important (lessons/pieces of wisdom/_____) in life?
630. What is the secret key to a highly (successful/happy/_____) life?
631. What are the best ways to achieve your (life goals/career goals/_____)?
632. How would you describe the most important (lesson/thing/_____) you have learned in life?
633. What do you believe is the (most/least/_____) rewarding experience you have gone through?

634. What is essential to (remember/forget/_____) when facing difficult times?
635. What do you think are the key ingredients to a (good/happy/_____) life?
636. How can someone achieve a (good/healthy/_____) life?
637. What are the (biggest/most common/_____) challenges to living a good life?
638. What (habits/values/_____) must one live by to enjoy a respectable life?
639. What important (relationship/experiences/_____) are necessary for a good life?
640. What is the most difficult (challenge/relationship/_____) you have faced in your life?
641. How did you work through a difficult (situation/friendship/_____)?
642. What did you learn from a challenging (experience/person/_____)?
643. How has a (problem/trial/_____) changed you for the better?
644. What (words of wisdom/advice/_____) would you give to someone going through a similar experience?
645. Did you take any steps to stay positive during the challenge?
646. How would you handle a (problem/challenging person/_____) differently if you could go back and do it again?

Chapter No. 43 - Questions to Ask Your Partner About Listening

647. Why is it important to listen to (others/yourself/_____)?

648. How do you make sure you are truly (listening/present/_____) to someone when she/he is speaking?

649. What do you do when you catch (yourself/me/_____) not paying attention to someone or zoning out?

650. Do you implement any techniques to (remember/forget/_____) what someone says?

651. How do you show me you are actively listening to me?

652. What action do you take when you don't understand what (someone/your children/_____) is saying?

653. What are the most important qualities of a (good/bad/_____) listener?

654. How do you feel when (your relatives/I/_____) actively listen to you?

655. How do you feel when I interrupt you when you are speaking?

656. How do you feel when (we/I/_____) try to solve your problems instead of just listening?

657. What do you do when you feel you need to understand (my/someone else's/_____) perspective?

658. What do you think are the most common (indicators/root causes/_____) of someone with bad listening skills?

659. How do bad listening skills negatively affect our relationship?

660. Are you satisfied with the way we (listen/respond/_____) to one another?

661. How does it make you feel when I listen to you without (judgment/really paying attention/_____)?

662. What are some steps (you/I/_____) can take to improve your listening skills?

663. What makes it difficult to be a good (listener/communicator/_____)?

Chapter No. 44 - Questions to Ask Your Partner About Love

664. What is your primary love language?
665. What do you think is the most important way to show me you (love/appreciate/_____) me?
666. What do you believe are the best ways to express love to your (family/friends/_____)?
667. What is an (underrated/unimportant/_____) way to show love?
668. How can you best receive love from (me/your family/_____)?
669. What are concrete ways to accept (love/friendship/_____)?
670. What is a love language that is (easy/difficult/_____) for you to use with me?
671. What are some manners you like to show (love/gratitude/_____) to others?
672. How do you feel when someone expresses love to you by using your love language?
673. How can you better handle someone expressing his/her (dislike/hate/_____) towards you?
674. How does it benefit our relationship if you (understand/embrace/_____) my love language?
675. What do you believe are the most common (mistakes/oversights/_____) people make when trying to show love?

676. What are signs of love language not being expressed (well/enough/_____) in our relationship?
677. What do you think are the most common (misused/overused/_____) love language behaviors?
678. How would not express love language appropriately affect our relationship?
679. What do you think are the (consequences/reasons/_____) of not using love languages in a relationship?
680. What is the healthiest way to address missing love languages in a relationship?

Chapter No. 45 - Questions to Ask Your Partner About Mindset

681. What do you think is the most important (opportunity/challenge/_____) of developing a positive mindset?
682. How do you stay motivated when life gets (challenging/easy/_____)?
683. What strategies do you implement to maintain (focus/productivity/_____) on your tasks?
684. How do you handle negative (thoughts/emotions/_____)?
685. To stay positive and optimistic, what do you (do/think about/_____)?
686. What is your advice on how to stay resilient in the face of adversity?
687. How do you develop a (creative/ inspired/_____) mindset?

688. What is the best approach to a (successful/new mindset/_____)?
689. How do you focus on your life goals?
690. What do you do when you feel (overwhelmed/unmotivated/_____) to become motivated again?
691. How do you implement successful time management and prioritize tasks?
692. What tricks do you suggest to stay productive when things (are challenging/get busy/_____)?
693. How can you keep track of your goals and hold yourself accountable?
694. What do you think are the main (causes/consequences/_____) of an unproductive mindset?
695. How do you think a (stagnant/negative/_____) mindset can be improved?
696. What actions have you taken in the past to help you become more (productive/resilient/_____)?
697. What are the biggest (obstacles/benefits/_____) to productivity in your life?
698. What benefits does a productive mindset offer?
699. How might having an unproductive mindset affect your (life/career/_____)?

Chapter No. 46 - Questions to Ask Your Partner About Money

700. What financial goals should we as partners set for the next (month/year/_____)?

701. What are your thoughts about our current (budget/expenditure/_____)?
702. Are there any areas in our lives where we could save more money?
703. How should we invest our money?
704. How do you feel about us having separate budgets?
705. How do you feel about our current situation regarding (debt/savings/_____)?
706. Are there any changes we should make to our (budget/savings/_____) to help us reach our financial goals?
707. What are our financial (goals/challenges/_____) for the next year?
708. How much money should we save each (month/year/_____) to reach our goals?
709. What are our biggest expenses, and how can we reduce them to save?
710. Are there any places where we can cut back on our spending?
711. What are (our/your/_____) priorities when we spend money?
712. Should we consider making any investments?
713. How can we ensure we are staying on track with our (budget/target savings/_____)?
714. How would you define our current financial (situation/goals/_____)?
715. What are both our short-term and long-term financial (goals/problems/_____)?
716. How can we plan to achieve our financial goals successfully?

717. What is our current budget and how can we best (improve/stick to/_____) it?
718. Are we on track to save enough for (retirement/next vacation/_____)?
719. Are we taking advantage of any tax breaks or deductions?
720. Do we have adequate (insurance/pension/_____)?
721. Are our (investments/savings/_____) being placed wisely?
722. What does your personal (monthly/yearly/_____) budget look like?
723. How do you track your personal spending?
724. What are your individual financial (goals/problems/_____)?
725. What is the best (approach/fix/_____) to saving money?
726. How do you prioritize your spending?
727. What are the biggest financial (challenges/opportunities/_____) you face?
728. What are the most important financial decisions we should make together?
729. How do you feel about incurring more debt?

Chapter No. 47 - Questions to Ask Your Partner About Motivation

730. What motivates you?
731. How do to stay motivated when you are feeling down?
732. What are the (most/least/_____) important factors to stay motivated?

733. What do you think are the biggest obstacles to prevent you from staying motivated?
734. What (strategies/procedures/_____) do you implement to become motivated?
735. How do you stay motivated when faced with (setbacks/failures/_____)?
736. How do you handle (distractions/temptations/_____) that may hinder your motivation?
737. What motivates you to stay focused and on track?
738. How do you measure your progress towards your (goals/outcome/_____)?
739. What do you do when you feel like (giving up/unhappy/_____)?
740. What type of (reward/space/_____) do you set aside for yourself after achieving your goals?
741. How do you approach motivation in relation to your (health/emotional well-being/_____)?
742. What do you do to stay (organized/on top/_____) of your task list?
743. What can you do to maintain your motivation over an extended period of time?

Chapter No. 48 - Questions to Ask Your Partner About Options

744. What options do you see are available to (us/you/_____)?
745. What are the pros and cons of each option?
746. What option is the (best/worst/_____) for us?
747. What are the risks associated with each option?

748. What do you believe are the potential rewards of each option?
749. What are the potential (cost/consequence/_____) of the option we want to pursue?
750. Which option is the most promising?
751. What makes this option the (most/least/_____) promising?
752. What are the potential (benefits/drawbacks/_____) of a promising option?
753. What do we need to consider most when evaluating this (promising/unfavorable/_____) option?
754. What steps are the (most/least/_____) appropriate to take when considering this option?
755. What would the largest (drawback/challenge/_____) of this option be?
756. What are the chances of this option (succeeding/failing/_____)?
757. Are there any more promising options than this one?
758. What is the (best/worst/_____) way for us to evaluate this option together?
759. What (risks/benefits/_____) are associated with this option?
760. How can we effectively handle those risks?

Chapter No. 49 - Questions to Ask Your Spouse About Parenting

761. What is the most important (thing/thought/_____) to remember while parenting?
762. How can we best (support/help/_____) each other as parents?

763. What do you believe is the (best/worst/_____) way to discipline our children?
764. How should we balance our children's needs with our own in a healthy way?
765. What do you think is the most essential lesson to teach our children?
766. How can we help our children (develop/improve/_____)?
767. What do you believe is the (best/worst/_____) way to handle this situation?
768. What can we do (together/separately/_____) to implement the right solution?
769. What does our child (need/don't need/_____) from us right now?
770. What can (you/we/_____) identify as the root cause of this issue?
771. What is our child trying to tell us?
772. How do you think we can help our child feel (safe/secure/_____)?
773. What are the (best/worst/_____) ways to handle our child's illness?
774. What do you believe is the optimal way to provide (comfort/care/_____) for our child when they are sick?
775. What are the most important things to keep in mind when our child is (sick/in problem/_____)?
776. How should we handle any potential medical emergencies?
777. What do you think are the best ways to keep our child (healthy/happy/_____)?
778. What is the most essential (quality/skill/_____) to being a good parent?

779. How can we support our children's (emotional/physiological/_____) needs effectively?
780. What is your ideal method of disciplining our children?
781. How can we foster our children's (independence/resilience/_____) as they grow?
782. What are the best ways to teach our children about (responsibility/discipline/_____)?
783. How do you think we could guide our children to develop healthy (relationships/mindset/_____)?
784. What do you identify as the biggest (mistake/success/_____) our parents made while raising us?
785. How did our parents' parenting styles affect (our/your/_____) relationships with them?
786. What do you believe our parents could have changed to improve our (childhoods/empathy/_____)?
787. How did the parenting styles of our parents shape our own (parenting styles/personalities/_____)?
788. What could our parents have done to better prepare us for (adulthood/life/_____)?

Chapter No. 50 - Questions to Ask Your Partner About Performance

789. What are the most important performance metrics to track in our relationship?
790. In what ways have you worked to improve (yourself/myself/_____) before?
791. What do you think are the biggest (challenges/reasons/_____) that stop you from performing better?

792. What (techniques/tools/_____) can we use to measure performance?

793. How do you motivate (yourself/me/_____) to be successful in performance?

794. What are the essential elements of a successful performance (review/chat/_____)?

795. What do you believe are the most important (qualities/traits/_____) for a successful relationship?

796. How can we best (support/motivate/_____) each other in our relationship?

797. What is necessary for us to focus on to maintain a (healthy/dynamic/_____) relationship?

798. What are the best ways to communicate our (needs/expectations/_____) to each other?

799. To have a (strong/lasting/_____) relationship, what are the key actions we must take?

Chapter No. 51 - Questions to Ask Your Partner About Priorities

800. What are the top three priorities in (your/my/_____) life?

801. How do you prioritize (your/our/_____) time efficiently?

802. In our family, what is the most important (part/aspect/_____) to focus on?

803. What should be prioritized above anything else (in our relationship/at home/_____)?

804. How do you decide about which (tasks/goals/_____) to prioritize above others?

805. What are some aspects of (your/my/_____) life that you could prioritize less?

806. How do you balance all your (priorities/objectives/_____)?

Chapter No. 52 - Questions to Ask Your Partner About Relationship Problems

807. What is the (root cause/consequences/_____) of our relationship problems?
808. How can we increase our (communication/appreciation/_____) with each other?
809. What can we do to rebuild (trust/love/_____) between us?
810. What are some (values/areas/_____) we should focus on to improve our relationship?
811. How can we ensure we both have our needs met?
812. What are the steps we can take to make our relationship (stronger/healthier/_____)?
813. How can we (better/healthily/_____) address our disagreements together?
814. How should we work on a (compromise/solution/_____) for the issues we face?
815. What can we do to (prevent/resolve/_____) conflicts in our relationship?
816. How can we best resolve (fights/conflicts/_____) when they arise?
817. What are the most important ways to show each other (love/appreciation/_____)?
818. How can we best support each other as (individuals/partners/_____)?

Chapter No. 53 - Questions to Ask Your Partner About Relationships

819. What do you (appreciate/like/_____) the most about our relationship?
820. What do you think is the most important (thing/activity/_____) we can do together to strengthen our relationship?
821. What do you believe are the best (ways/manner/_____) to show one another love and affection?
822. What is the most important thing we can (do/say/_____) to stay connected?
823. What one thing do you think is essential for us to (create/foster/_____) a healthy relationship?
824. What do you believe makes a relationship (successful/work/_____)?
825. What is the most important (part/quality/_____) of a relationship?
826. How do you approach (disagreements/fights/_____) in a relationship?
827. What do you think is the key to keeping a relationship (healthy/joyful/_____)?
828. What do you look for as the most important (qualities/attributes/_____) in a partner?
829. How do you show your (care/affection/_____) to your partner?
830. What do you think is the best way to (communicate/talk/_____ effectively?
831. What are the least significant (qualities/traits/_____) to a successful relationship?

832. How should couples work through (disagreements/arguments/_____) together?
833. What do you believe is the best way to show (appreciation/love/_____) for your partner?
834. How should couples communicate with each other?
835. What do you think are the essentials to keep in mind for (relationships/avoiding breakups/_____)?
836. What do you believe are the biggest (challenges/opportunities/_____) couples face in their relationships?
837. What can be the biggest warning signs that a relationship is (unhealthy/in jeopardy/_____)?
838. What are the major red flags that a relationship will not work out?
839. What were the largest (mistakes/oversights/_____) you made in a previous relationship?
840. What do you identify as the (main/worst/_____) mistakes that your partner made in that relationship?
841. What do you think were the primary communication challenges in that relationship?
842. What do you believe are the essential qualities for a healthy relationship to (grow/stay strong/_____)?
843. How would you define communication's importance in a relationship?
844. In resolving conflicts in a relationship, what is most important for (you/me/_____) to remember?
845. How do you think trust impacts a healthy relationship?
846. What do you believe is imperative to keep in mind when you express your (feelings/concerns/_____) in a relationship?

847. Have you been in an (unhealthy/unhappy/_____) relationship before?

848. What do you see as some of the warning signs in a (toxic/unhealthy/_____) relationship?

849. How would you leave a (bad/challenging/_____) relationship?

850. What could you learn from the experience of being in a bad relationship?

851. What advice would you give to someone who is currently in an (unhealthy/unhappy/_____) relationship?

852. From your experience, what are the most important aspects of a healthy relationship?

853. What would you identify as the biggest red flag in an unhealthy relationship?

854. What do you appreciate the (most/least/_____) about our relationship?

855. What would you like to do together to make our relationship (stronger/healthier/_____)?

856. What do you think we need to work on above anything else in our relationship?

857. What do you see as the best (thing/accomplishment/_____) we have done together as a couple?

858. What do you believe is most essential to keeping our relationship (healthy/happy/_____)?

Chapter No. 54 - Questions to Ask Your Partner About Responsibilities

859. What responsibilities do you (have/enjoy/_____) in our relationship that are the most important?

860. How can we best divide up our (shared/individual/_____) responsibilities so that we both feel supported?
861. What are essential responsibilities that we both (share/dislike/_____)?
862. What is the best method of communicating our (responsibilities/errors/_____) to each other?
863. What are the most important responsibilities that you have to (yourself/our family/_____)?
864. What are some of the (responsibilities/privileges/_____) that we have as individuals?
865. How can we fulfill our responsibilities to our (families/friends /_____)?
866. Do we have any obligation to our (environment/community/_____)?
867. How can we successfully use our (resources/money/_____) to ensure that we are fulfilling our responsibilities to the planet?
868. How do you delegate (responsibilities/tasks/_____) to others?
869. What are some of the most challenging responsibilities you have (managed/not done/_____)?
870. How do you handle the stress of taking on (new/old/_____) responsibilities?
871. How do you take responsibility for your actions and decisions?
872. What actions do you take when you feel (overwhelmed/guilty/_____) by your obligations?
873. How do you prioritize your tasks when you take on multiple challenging responsibilities?

874. In what ways do you take responsibility for (mistakes/failures/_____)?

Chapter No. 55 - Questions to Ask Your Partner About Romance

875. What is the most (romantic/sexy/_____) thing you've ever done for someone?
876. What do you remember as the most romantic gesture someone has ever done for you?
877. What do you believe is the most (romantic/sexy/_____) thing you could give to someone?
878. Is there an ideal romantic gesture someone could do for (you/me/_____)?
879. What is the most romantic thing you can do for your partner to show your (love/desire/_____)?
880. What do you love the most about (me/yourself/_____)?
881. What is your favorite memory of us together?
882. What makes our relationship (special/lovely/_____)?
883. What do you believe is the most (important/repulsive/_____) part of a romantic relationship?
884. What is the key to a (successful/romantic/_____) relationship?
885. What is a memorable (romantic/adventurous/_____) thing I have done for you?
886. What is your favorite (romantic/passionate/_____) activity that we do together?
887. How do you define romance?
888. How can we (ignite/keep/_____) the spark alive in our relationship?

889. What is your favorite romance movie? Why?
890. What is your favorite song about romance? Why?
891. Where is the most romantic place you have ever visited?
892. What is the (most/least/_____) romantic gift you have received?
893. When you remember the most romantic things you've ever said to someone, what were they?
894. What would the most (romantic/sexy/_____) words be that I could say to you?
895. What do you believe is the most romantic thing you can say to someone?
896. How important are regular (date nights/alone time/_____) in a relationship for you?
897. What do you think is the best way to show someone you care for them romantically?

Chapter No. 56 - Questions to Ask Your Partner About Safety

898. What do we need to put in place to protect our (health/well-being/_____)?
899. How can we make sure our things are safe while we are away?
900. Are there any (safety/health/_____) concerns we should be aware of?
901. What safety measures should we take while arguing?
902. What are our natural disaster safety plans?
903. How can we create a safe space to talk about our (feelings/problems/_____) openly?

904. What do you need me to provide to help you feel emotionally (secure/better/_____)?
905. How can I support you when you are feeling (overwhelmed/unhappy/_____)?
906. What do you do for self-care when you are feeling down?
907. How can I help you feel more (confident/comfortable/_____) expressing your emotions to me?
908. What (burdens/responsibilities/_____) can I take off from you now?
909. In what ways can I (support/encourage/_____) you right now?
910. How can I create a safe and secure environment for (us/our family/_____)?
911. What do you think would lead us to better (communication/relationship/_____)?
912. How can we resolve (conflicts/arguments/_____) more effectively and efficiently?
913. What can we do to increase our (emotional intimacy/love/_____) between us?
914. What do you think would help us strengthen our relationship?

Chapter No. 57 - Questions to Ask Your Partner About Self-Esteem

915. What are some things that make you feel (unworthy/worthy/_____)?
916. How can you (recognize/challenge/_____) negative thoughts about yourself?

917. What are some positive (affirmations/things/_____) you used to address your feelings of unworthiness?

918. What steps do you take to learn how to accept compliments and recognize your worth?

919. What are some healthy ways you cope with feelings of (unworthiness/sadness/_____)?

920. What is an (optimum/subpar/_____) way for me to communicate your worth to you?

921. What are some (practical/impractical/_____) steps you can take to build your self-esteem?

922. In what ways should you (recognize/celebrate/_____) your successes?

923. What are your favorite ways to practice self-care?

924. How important is it for you to forgive yourself for past mistakes and move forward?

Chapter No. 58 - Questions to Ask Your Partner About Sex

925. What do you find most (pleasurable/ unsatisfactory/_____) about sex?

926. What do you (like/not like/_____) about our sex life?

927. What can we do to (improve/spice up/_____) our sex life?

928. What are the most important elements of a satisfying sexual experience for you?

929. What do we need to (keep in mind/forget/_____) regarding sex?

930. What are some changes you'd like to make to our sex life?

931. Do you feel (comfortable/uncomfortable/_____) with the current level of our physical intimacy?
932. Are there any (elements/toys/_____) you would like to add to our intimate life?
933. How can we make our sex life more (exciting/fulfilling/_____)?
934. What would make our sex life more (spontaneous/romantic/_____)?
935. What can we do to (increase/enhance/_____) intimacy in our sex life?

Chapter No. 59 - Questions to Ask Your Partner About the Future

936. When you picture yourself in (five/ten/_____) years, where are you and what are you doing?
937. What do you expect to be the biggest (challenge/issue/_____) you will face in the future?
938. What do you think will be the most (rewarding/exciting/_____) thing in the future?
939. Do you have a prediction about what the biggest (change/disruption/_____) in the world in the next decade will be?
940. What will be the most important (skill/mindset/_____) to have in the future?
941. What would you identify are the largest (threats/opportunity/_____) to a successful future?
942. What do you believe are the most (pressing/concerning/_____) issues that should be addressed today?

943. What are the next steps we can take as a society to prevent negative (repercussions/feelings/_____) in the future?
944. What are the most effective ways to combat (climate change/poverty/_____)?
945. How can our society best ensure (economic stability/peace?
946. What do you think our future together holds?
947. What future (goals/threats/_____) do you have for us to focus on?
948. How important is family and having (children/grandchildren/_____) to you in the future?
949. How do you see us handling finances and building our assets together?
950. How do you envision our future (living arrangements/lifestyle/_____)?

Chapter No. 60 - Questions to Ask Your Partner About the Past

951. What is your (favorite/worst/_____) memory of your childhood?
952. What was your favorite school (subject/class/_____)?
953. Where was your first job and what did you do?
954. What difficult (experience/person/_____) shaped you during your childhood years?
955. What is the (best/worst/_____) decision you have ever made?
956. What would you say is the most important lesson you learned from your (parents/grandparents/_____)?

957. What is your most (embarrassing/exciting/_____) memory?
958. What is the most (adventurous/silly/_____) thing you have done?

Chapter No. 61 - Questions to Ask Your Partner When He or She is Mad or Unhappy

959. How can I best help you feel (better/happier/_____)?
960. What do you need from (me/your family/_____) to help?
961. Is there anything I can do to improve this situation?
962. What steps can we take to help us (resolve/avoid/_____) this issue?
963. How can I best show my (care/appreciation/_____) for your feelings?
964. Is there a way that I can make this easier for (you/us/_____)?
965. What can I (offer/do/_____) to help you feel better?
966. Can you explain what has angered you?
967. What can I do to help (you/us/_____)?
968. What can I do to improve this (issue/argument/_____)?
969. How can I show my care to you?
970. What do you need me to (do/say/_____) right now?
971. Is there something I said or did that (upset/concern/_____) you?
972. Can we talk about this issue calmly?
973. What do you need right now to feel better?
974. What can I do (at this moment/next time/_____) to help you feel better?

975. What would you like from me (right now/next time/_____)?
976. Is there any way I can improve this situation?
977. How can I help you to relax?
978. What do you think are some (steps/ideas/_____) to help us resolve this issue?
979. Is there something I didn't say or didn't do that angered you?
980. How can I best show you I care about how you are (feeling/thinking/_____)?
981. What's wrong?
982. What can I do to help?
983. How can I stop making you feel (unhappy/anxious/_____)?
984. What (steps/decisions/_____) can I take to make this better between us?
985. What can I do to show my care and affection for (you/our relationship/_____)?
986. What can I do to support you better?
987. Is there anything I can do to better show my (appreciation/love/_____) for you?

Chapter No. 62 - Questions to Ask Your Partner About You

988. What is my greatest (strength/weakness/_____)?
989. What do you believe is my biggest (weakness/contribution/_____)?
990. What are some simple ways that I can (improve/challenge/_____) myself?

991. What do you think should be my primary (focus/concern/_____) to reach my goals?
992. What should I work on to become a better (person/communicator/_____)?
993. How can I become more (successful/humble/_____)?
994. What do I do (best/badly/_____)?
995. What do you appreciate the (most/least/_____) about me?
996. What are my (qualities/inadequacies/_____)?
997. What can I do to continually improve myself?
998. How can I help make our relationship (stronger/trustworthy/_____)?
999. What do you believe I could do to improve our (communication/arguments/_____)?
1000. What are some ways I can make our time together more (enjoyable/naughty/_____).